# The Wasp in the Mug

## Unforgettable Irish Proverbs

D1260138

# The Wasp in the Mug

## Unforgettable Irish Proverbs

**Newly Translated from the Irish by**

**Gabriel Rosenstock**

# Mercier Press

**Mercier Press**
PO Box 5, 5 French Church Street, Cork *and*
24 Lower Abbey Street, Dublin 1.

Text © Gabriel Rosenstock, 1993
Illustrations © Pieter Sluis, 1993

ISBN 1 85635 043 6

A CIP catalogue record for this book is available from the
British Library.

*To all who keep these proverbs alive!*

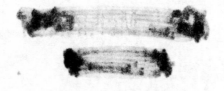

Printed in Ireland by Colour Books Ltd.

# Preface

The wit and wisdom of the Gael are tightly packed in the proverb. Irish proverbs elucidate the Irish mind in a distilled fashion, frequently throwing light on aspects of social and cultural history. Certain media mandarins who question the very existence of 'an Irish mind' are themselves, generally, unfamiliar with native lore.

'Ba é chéad bhia ar an sliogán dó na scéalta sin' means 'he was nurtured on those tales'. But look how the Irish language concretises things – a great boon in this age of linguistic obfuscation: literally it says 'the first food on the shell for him was those tales'. The image of the shell (used as a plate) springs to the visual mind immediately.

Traditionally, the Gaelic mind has abhorred abstractions so that abstract truths are represented here by metaphor and simile, drawn from the natural world. That natural world is one of endless variety. Thus, in Irish a potato isn't just a potato. Munster people say *práta* (prawtha) and Connaught people say *fata*, giving rise to the observation that the Connaught people would have washed, boiled and eaten their potatoes by the time it took the Munster people to say *práta!*

But what about *falcaire*, an old seed-potato, or a dried up one, used to describe a deceptive person! *Prochán* is a potato roasted in ashes – or a podgy person. *Sliomach* is a soft potato or a spineless individual. *Creachán*, a small potato or a puny person.

The proverbial mind, therfore, creeps into single words, investing them with praise, derision or whatever. One word, *stadhan*, decribes a flock of birds over a shoal of fish. One word, *gabhgaire*, describes an onlooker at a game of cards. The word *canúnaí* means someone interested in or addicted to dialect. Where else in the world would you find such an addiction!

I have read nature poetry, proverbs and weather lore to inner-city children who have never seen a frog, or a heron, or touched bog-cotton or enjoyed the aroma of turf. And yet teachers and librarians assure me that their minds are fired by wildlife, as if some ancient memory of mountains and the sea still lingers on in the genetic pool. Fanciful? Perhaps.

The mind which created these proverbs no longer exists in its full integrity: the language is thinning out, where it has not actually been stilled, and with this loss comes a less sophisticated response to the diversity of nature and an impoverished nomenclature. But we can absorb that mind, to a lesser or greater degree. At least a hundred of these proverbs are a living part of my own consciousness, my mental furniture. Their usefulness is not merely by way of repartee. In a way they form the groundwork for a mental Ninja-culture, an adroitness, a sharpness always to hand when the dross and morass of contemporary culture threaten to stifle us, utterly.

Irish is no mere folksy language of quaint expressions. It has the oldest, most sophisticated literature in Western Europe. To this day 80 or so books are published, yearly, in Irish. Many see the language in a state of inevitable decline. Estimates of the number of native speakers sometimes fall below the 20,000 mark.

It would be a tragedy beyond words if the Irish language disappeared, and those of us who know and love the language would not wish to see one single word perish. *Floreat!*

### Note on the Translations

In many cases I have gone for a rhyme in English. This lengthens the phrase, in some instances, with a slight change of colour or emphasis. Here and there I have added a comment or interpretation, not superfluously, I hope. The selection is a personal one, proverbs I have noted, or heard, and enjoyed over a period of twenty years or so.

*Gabriel Rosenstock*
*Baile Átha Cliath*

# Arrangement

The arrangement might seem haphazard or arbitrary to some readers. I have deliberately chosen to avoid repetitiveness and decided against grouping proverbs under various thematic headings – food, drink, old age etc. Think of this collection as a bag of liquorice all-sorts. Dip in, now and again, when you feel the urge. Don't keep them all to yourselves. They're for sharing.

I have invented titles for quite a few proverbs, simply to avoid the sameness of typography throughout, so don't be surprised if you come across such tabloid headlines as *The Curse of the Leprechaun!*

# The Wasp in the Mug

Na trí súile is géire:
    Súil na circe i ndiaidh an ghráinne,
    Súil an ghabha i ndiaidh an tairne,
    Agus súil ainnire i ndiaidh a grá gil.

\*\*\*

D'fheannfadh sé dreancaid ar a craiceann.

\*\*\*

Caora mhór an t-uan i bhfad.

\*\*\*

Cuid an daimh den eadra.

\*\*\*

Cosúlacht báis sop i ndiaidh na circe.

\*\*\*

Ní baol don bhacach an gadaí.

\*\*\*

Ní féidir fear gan ceann a chrochadh.

\*\*\*

The three sharpest eyes:
   The hen's eye on the grain,
   The blacksmith's eye on the nail,
   The loving eyes of a maid.

\*\*\*

He'd flay a flea for its skin.[1]

\*\*\*

To carry a lamb is no great load
   But it's a sheep you'll have a mile down the road.

\*\*\*

The ox's part in the milking operations.[2]

\*\*\*

A wisp of straw on a hen's rear:
   Death will come in a day and a year.[3]

\*\*\*

The beggar need not fear the thief.

\*\*\*

### A Headless Man!

You cannot hang a headless man.

---

[1] Meanness.

[2] Might be said of you when you're completely unconcerned with proceedings.

[3] A superstition, to be ignored at your peril.

Sceitheann fíon fírinne.

Truth is spilled
  When wine is swilled.

Is goirt iad na deora, na deora a siltear
   Ach is goirte go mór iad na deora nach siltear.

*\*\**

Ná bí abhus is a bheith thall
   Ná bí thall is a bheith abhus –
   Nó má bhíonn tú abhus is a bheith thall,
   Ní bheidh tú thall ná abhus.

*\*\**

Cnuasach na gráinneoige.

*\*\**

Gach breac mar a shnámhann ach an scadán ar a dhrom.

*\*\**

Sin méadú ort! arsa an dreoilín
   Nuair a rinne sé a mhún san fharraige.

*\*\**

Mar a dúirt an gabhar bacach – ní fheadar
   Cé acu is fearr luas nó moilleas.

*\*\**

**'Tears, idle tears, I know not what they mean...'**

Bitter the tears, the tears that are shed,
    Bitterer those that remain in the head.

\*\*\*

Don't be here when you should be there
    Don't be there when you should be here
    Because if you're here and there
    You won't be anywhere.[4]

\*\*\*

### Amnesia

He gathers and he gathers and he hides his store away –
    But where the hell he put it, the hedgehog cannot say.

\*\*\*

Every fish as it swims, but the herring on its back.[5]

\*\*\*

There now, you're bigger! – said the wren to the sea,
    (Having done a pee...)

\*\*\*

As the lame goat said: I don't know
    Which is the better, to go fast or slow.

\*\*\*

---

[4] This one can be used to spare somebody a trip to India to see his guru again.

[5] How to cut a fish.

Bean ag gol, bean ag gáire,
  Bean eile agus a cuid putóg lena sáile,
  Cé acu sin an bhean is mó náire?
  Is é sin an bhean a bhíos ag gáire.


\*\*\*


Glór foiche i muga.

\*\*\*



Imíonn an méanfach ó dhuine go duine
  Mar a imíonn an spideog ó bhile go bile.


\*\*\*


Bainne cíche circe a bhleán
  In adhairc mhuice
  Agus a mheascadh le cleite cait.


\*\*\*


Bean mhic is máthair chéile
  Mar a bheadh cat is luch in aghaidh a chéile.


\*\*\*


Ní beag a bheith go dona, ach gan a bheith go dona faoi.


\*\*\*

A woman with tears in her eyes, a woman with a
    laughing face,
  A woman with her guts strewn all over the place,
  Which of these most disgraces her race?
  She with the laughing face![6]

***

The voice of a wasp in a mug.[7]

***

### Yawn

A yawn can pass from you to me
    Like a robin, from tree to tree.

***

Breastmilk from a hen
  Milked into a pig's horn
  And stirred with a cat's feather.[8]

***

The son's wife and the mother-in-law,
  Cat and mouse, tooth and claw!

***

It's bad enough being miserable without being miserable
    about it.

---

[6] The reference to entrails should be understood in the context of Ireland's gory history.

[7] Say this of a small nasty person.

[8] A cure for what ails you.

'Beidh mise i bpáirt leat,'
  Mar a dúirt an sionnach leis an gcoileach.

***

Síol don phiast agus síol don chág
  Síol chun lofa agus síol chun fáis.

***

Lán gabhála de ghainimh trá
  Lán mála den ghaoith aduaidh
  Comhairle a thabhairt do mhnaoi bhoirb
  Nó buille ribe ar iarann fuar.

***

Is fearr fuíoll fonóide ná fuíoll formaid.

***

Uan dubh ar dtús,
  Searrach is a thóin leat,
  Cuach i dtaobh na cluaise clí,
  Is ní éireoidh an bhliain leat.

***

Nuair a lasfaidh tú déanfaidh tú tine,
  Arsa an sionnach nuair a chac sé ar an sneachta.

***

'Let's be partners, old stock!'
  Said the fox to the cock.

\*\*\*

A seed for the worm, a seed for the crow,
  A seed to rot and a seed to sow.

\*\*\*

**With apologies to all feminists ...**

Put sense into a woman's mind?
  Try filling a bag with the north wind!
  Try carrying an armful of sand from the shore
  Or beating cold iron with a little rib of hair.

\*\*\*

Better by far to be laughed at a lot
  Than be envied by all for the little you've got.

\*\*\*

A black lamb in front of you,
  A foal that turns his rear to you,
  A cuckoo in your left ear,
  It will be a bad year![9]

\*\*\*

You'll light up soon and you'll glow,
  Said the fox who shat in the snow.[10]

---

[9] Just in case you're worried, all these omens are supposed to occur more or less at the same time.

[10] A spouse or flat-mate might utter this at your miserable attempts at making a fire.

# THE WASP IN THE MUG

Cuir síoda ar ghabhar agus is gabhar i gcónaí é.

***

Ceann círtha a dhíolas na cosa.

***

Sháraigh na mná Harry Stottle
  Is sháraigh Harry Stottle an diabhal.

***

Tá cluasa fada ar mhuca beaga.

***

Cuileog an chairn aoiligh is mó a ghníos torann.

***

Trí shórt ban nach féidir le fear a dtuiscint:
  Bean óg
  Bean mheánaosta
  Seanbhean.

***

An rud nach bhfuil is nach mbeidh,
  Nead ag an luch i bhféasóg an chait.

***

A goat is a goat, goat born and bred
    Though you clothe him in silk from hoof to head.

\*\*\*

Good grooming, with hair kept neat –
    Whatever your faults – will keep you on your feet.

\*\*\*

Women were too much for Aristotle
    And Aristotle was too much for the devil.

\*\*\*

Little pigs have big ears.[11]

\*\*\*

The fly on the dung-heap is the noisiest of all.

\*\*\*

Three types of women a man can't understand:
    A young woman
    A middle-aged woman
    An old woman.

\*\*\*

### The Cat's Whiskers

Something that never will be – and that, my friend, is
    that –
    The nest of a mouse in the whiskers of a cat.

---

[11] Children hear more than we realise.

Tabhair do phóg do chois an ghiorria.

Kiss the leg of a hare![12]

[12] Say goodbye to something lost forever.

Tá a spuir féin agus capall duine eile aige.

***

Caill do chlú agus faigh arís é,
   Agus ní hé an rud céanna é.

***

Bean bhreá, nó capall bán, nó tigh ar ardán,
   Sin trí mhallacht an chlutharacháin.

***

Ní sheasann sac folamh.

***

Scinneann gráinne ón scilligeadh.

***

Na trí glórtha is binne:
   Meilt bhró, géimneach bó is béic linbh.

***

Na trí rian is giorra a fhanas:
   Rian éin ar chraoibh,
   Rian bric ar linn,
   Rian fir ar mhnaoi.

***

He has his own spurs and another man's horse.

\*\*\*

## Good Name

Lose your good name,
   Regain it – it's never the same again.

\*\*\*

## The Curse of the Leprechaun!

A beautiful woman, a white horse, a house on a height:
   The curse of the leprechaun! What a fright!

\*\*\*

An empty sack won't stand.[13]

\*\*\*

A grain escapes from the shelling.[14]

\*\*\*

Three sounds that are sweetest:
   Quernstone grinding, cow lowing, child screaming.

\*\*\*

Three traces soon gone:
   On a branch – a bird,
   In a pool – a trout,
   On a woman – a man.

---

[13] It's hard to work on an empty stomach.

[14] Every community has its own odd-ball, or genius.

Ná trí héisc is mire:
  rotha,
  ranga,
  agus rón.

***

Na trí beaga is fearr –
  Beag na coirceoige
  Beag na gcaorach
  Agus beag na mná.

***

An fhaid a bheidh naosc ar móin is gob uirthi.

***

Teachtaire an fhiaigh ón Áirc.

***

Is mór an náire do Mháire Ní Dhálaigh
  A bheith ar deireadh, a bheith ar deireadh.

***

The fastest in the sea:
   The ray,
   The mackerel,
   And the seal.[15]

\*\*\*

### The Little Woman

The best of the littlest –
   The little hive
   The little sheep
   The little woman.

\*\*\*

### Saecula Saeculorum

As long as the snipe on the moor has a beak.[16]

\*\*\*

Hark! Hark! The raven-messenger of the Ark.[17]

\*\*\*

### No shame

Mary Daly, have you no shame?
   Last again, last again![18]

---

[15] The Irish actually says the three fastest *fish*. The seal is not a fish but takes its place in the triad by dint of alliteration!

[16] Forever.

[17] The slow messenger who never returns.

[18] Children used to say this to the last straggling crow, which often had the effect of the crow getting into another gear and maybe even heading the posse!

Bean mar mhuic
    Bean mar chirc
    Bean mar chaora.

***

Sceinneann éan as gach ealta.

***

Nuair a chacann gé cacann siad go léir.

***

Spáráil na circe fraoigh ar an bhfraoch.

***

Ní haon mhoill ar fhaoilleán
    Nuair a thagann an scadán.

***

Is maith an chearc nach mbeireann amuigh.

***

An chearc ar fad is an anraith.

***

Piggish woman
  Hennish woman
  Sheepish woman.[19]

***

From the flock in the sky one bird will fly.[20]

***

Let one goose shit and they're all at it.[21]

***

The moorhen sparing the heather.[22]

***

Herring in sight,
  Seagull in full flight.

***

Good the hen that lays within.[23]

***

The whole hen and the soup.[24]

---

[19] Not quite as piggish as it sounds: natural metaphors for stubborness, flightiness and docility!

[20] Not necessarily a black sheep, mind you!

[21] Applicable to 'dedicated followers of fashion'.

[22] Unnecessary parsimoniousness. It is said that the moorhen only eats what's between her feet.

[23] A warning not to be ostentatious.

[24] The lot – the whole shooting gallery.

Ubh na circe duibhe.

***

Níor thacht an bia riamh máthair na sicíní.

***

Ó bearradh na rónta.

***

Dála an mhadarua agus na silíní.

***

Bhearrfadh sé luch ina chodladh.

***

Ló go n-oíche an luch.

***

The black hen's egg.[25]

\*\*\*

Food never choked a mother of chickens.[26]

\*\*\*

### Shearing seals

Before you were born,
  When seals were shorn ... [27]

\*\*\*

Like the fox and the cherries.[28]

\*\*\*

He'd shave a sleeping mouse!

\*\*\*

### Sex-life

The mouse is a fright –
  From morning to night![29]

\*\*\*

---

[25] Something prized, though not deservedly so.

[26] The poor selfless creature is left with slim pickings.

[27] A time no one remembers.

[28] When he couldn't get his paws on them he declared they were sour.

[29] A reference to the mouse's prodigious sex-life and, by imputation, to any Casanova – or maenad.

Fear óg diagaithe ábhar diabhail seanduine.

# THE WASP IN THE MUG

A pious young man – he'd move you to tears –
A randy old divil in later years.

Tá an earc luachra ina bholg.

\*\*\*

Codladh an ghiorria.

\*\*\*

Fear na caorach beirithe.

\*\*\*

Is olc an banbh ascall agat é.

\*\*\*


Aicearra an chait tríd an ngríosaigh.

\*\*\*

Fuadach an chait ar an domlas.

\*\*\*

The newt is in his belly.[30]

\*\*\*

The sleep of the hare.[31]

\*\*\*

He boiled his sheep.[32]

\*\*\*

It's a bad piglet you've under your arm.[33]

\*\*\*

**Ouch!**

The cat's shortcut through the embers.[34]

\*\*\*

The cat chasing the uneatable.[35]

---

[30] It was believed that if you slept outside the newt would invade you and gobble up your food as fast as you were swallowing it.

[31] One eye open! The hare looms large in oral Irish literature. A saying I was much taken by, when I first visited the Dingle peninsula, was *chomh scaipthe le mún giorria* – as scattered as a hare's piss. The animal, seemingly, urinates on the run.

[32] He had a great feast but was left with no sheep.

[33] Someone who might turn on you after having done him a good deed.

[34] When it's best not to cut corners.

[35] He's caught a Tartar! Reminds me a bit of the definition of a university professor – the unsackable teaching the unteachable, or the huntsman – the unspeakable in pursuit of the uneatable! Word-play in Irish, however, rarely relies on punning, spoonerisms and the like. The notorious 'Irish bull' – a ludicrous blunder – may have come from language-shift, from Irish to English, as when the returned Yank, distressed to see the pig in the kitchen, exclaimed: 'Extinguish that pig at once!'

# THE WASP IN THE MUG

Tógfaidh dath dubh ach ní thógfaidh dubh dath.

***

Ní dheachaidh Harry Stottle amach ar oíche fhómhair.

***

Báisteach ó Dhia chugainn is gan é bheith fliuch
Is cuid an lae amárach go ndéana sé anocht.

***

Lá millte na móna, lá fómhair an chabáiste.

***

Is í an dias is troime is ísle a chromann a ceann.

***

Bí bog crua ar nós eireaball na bó.

***

Colour will take black but black will not take colour.[36]

\*\*\*

### Harry Stottle!

Aristotle never went out on an autumn night.[37]

\*\*\*

### Rain

Rain from God and let it be light
  And may tomorrow's share come down tonight.

\*\*\*

Turf ruined, cabbage harvested.[38]

\*\*\*

The heaviest ear of corn bends lowest.[39]

\*\*\*

### Sacred Cows

Be soft and hard like the cow's tail.[40]

---

[36] Easier to blacken someone's reputation than to restore it.

[37] Various eminences, Aristotle, Dean Swift, Cromwell, Julia of Norwich, Henry the Eighth, Napoleon, as well as a host of Irish poets, most notably Eoghan Rua Ó Súilleabháin, have found their way, for different reasons, to the Gaelic pantheon of Immortals.

[38] A rainy day, bad for turf, good for cabbage.

[39] Humility in the great.

[40] Dealing with people.

Téann an bainne sa gheimhreadh go hadharca na mbó.

***

Gheobhair in aoileach na Bealtaine é!

***

Ceathrar sagart gan a bheith santach,
  Ceathrar Francach gan a bheith buí,
  Ceathrar gréasaí gan a bheith bréagach –
  Sin dhá fhear déag nach bhfuil sa tír.

***

Is fearr seo é ná cá bhfuil sé.

***

Chomh leitheadach leis na cuacha.

***

Chomh Gaelach le muca Dhroichead Átha.

***

In winter the milk goes to the horns of the cow.[41]

\*\*\*

### Lost and found

It's lost, you say?
　　You'll find it in the dung of May.

\*\*\*

### Dirty dozen

Four priests that are not greedy,
　　Four Frenchmen that are not tanned,
　　Four cobblers not deceitful –
　　A dozen you won't find in the land.

\*\*\*

Better 'Here it is!' than 'Where is it?'

\*\*\*

### Comparisons ...

As conceited as the cuckoos.

\*\*\*

As Irish as the pigs of Drogheda.

---

[41] The cow has been so dominant in Ireland that she is Ireland herself – 'silk of the kine', *Droimeann Donn Dílis*. Our sacred river, the Boyne/Bóinn means 'fair cow' and is linguistically cognate with the Sanscrit, *Govinda*, another name for *Krishna*. However, the Indo-European question is a minefield. We do not have a modern etymological dictionary in Irish to tell us that the word for a road, *bóthar*, is related to *bó*, a cow – the width to allow one cow to pass another.

Chomh dubh le tóin an phúca.

***

Chomh géar-radharcach le gainéad.

***

Chomh díreach is atá an chnámh i ndroim na lachan.

***

Chomh dall ar meisce le coinín.

***

Chomh nata le frog san fhómhar.

***

Chomh bocht le bairneach.

***

Chomh bréan le pluais an mhadarua.

***

As black as the Pooka's arse![42]

\*\*\*

As sharp-sighted as a gannet.[43]

\*\*\*

As straight as a bone in the back of a duck.

\*\*\*

As blind drunk as a rabbit.[44]

\*\*\*

As swollen as a frog in autumn.

\*\*\*

As poor as a limpet.

\*\*\*

As smelly as the fox's den.

---

[42] The pooka was a dominant elemental in Irish life. One researcher, Deasún Breatnach, is of the opinion that the word may be related to the Greek *psyche*, in which the *y* is sounded much like a *u*. The Liffey has its origins in *Poll an Phúca* (the Pooka's Hole). The *púca na sméar* for instance, or berry-pooka, was responsible for the blight on berries in the autumn. The pooka is as large as life in Flann O'Brien's classic novel, *At Swim-Two-Birds*.

[43] Ireland has one of the most important gannet colonies in Europe, situated in the enchanting Skelligs.

[44] I must say I've never heard this one. In Dunquin, Co. Kerry, the lovely comparison used was that of the 'caobach', a sea-bird known to stand on one leg on a rock some distance from the shore! Thus, 'bhí caobach air' – he was mad drunk!

Staying with ornithological imagery I once saw five pints of stout perched on a counter and a local wit observed: *Féach na fiaigh mhara* – 'would you look at the ravens!'

Chomh caoch le bonn mo bhróige.

\*\*\*

Chomh casta le hadharc gabhair.

\*\*\*

Fiach nó iascach ní raibh air riamh an rath,
   Ach an té a leanann béal an chéachta ní folamh a
    bheidh a shac!

\*\*\*

Dála reithe Sheáin na Buile!

\*\*\*

B'fhearr liom a bheith ag fáscadh gainimhe faoi
   m'fhiacla.

\*\*\*

Faoi mar a chacfadh an t-asal é!

\*\*\*

Chomh trom sin go n-íosfá le spúnóg é.

\*\*\*

As blind as the sole of my shoe.

\*\*\*

As twisted as a goat's horn.

\*\*\*

Hunting and fishing never bring luck –
Follow the plough and earn an honest buck![45]

\*\*\*

Like Mad John's ram![46]

\*\*\*

I'd rather crunch sand under my teeth.

\*\*\*

As the donkey would evacuate it![47]

\*\*\*

You could eat it with a spoon it's so heavy.[48]

\*\*\*

---

[45] Said of those too fond of idle pleasures and aping the gentry.

[46] John used to bring the ram to Cahirciveen, not to sell – as you might think –
but as an excuse to go on a batter. The ram got so accustomed to this pilgrimage
that he'd make his own way home.

[47] Said of something that's just right – say, an appropriate gift!

[48] Fog.

Chomh sleamhain le bolg eascún.

\*\*\*

Chomh tiubh le tiul.

\*\*\*

Chomh pioctha le sagart.

\*\*\*

Chomh ramhar le ministir.

\*\*\*

Chomh sámh le liopadaileap.

\*\*\*


Bás Aoine,
    Tórramh Sathairn
    Agus sochraid Domhnaigh.

\*\*\*

Bíonn ceathanna sneachta um Bhealtaine
    Agus cailleacha ar leabaidh ag srantarnaigh
    Agus mairbh ag tarraingt ar theampallaibh.

\*\*\*

As slippery as an eel's belly.

\*\*\*

Like a hail of bullets.

\*\*\*

As neat as a priest.

\*\*\*

As plump as a vicar.

\*\*\*

As tranquil as a basking shark.

\*\*\*

### Exit!

Friday death,
   Saturday wake,
   Sunday funeral.[49]

\*\*\*

Snow falling in May,
   Hags snoring in bed all day
   And the dead being carted to the grave.

\*\*\*

---

[49] The traditionally preferred way to go.

'Is deas í an ghlaineacht,' arsa an sraoill
Is í ag glanadh an phláta le heireaball an chait.

'Cleanliness is a nice thing', said the slattern,
Cleaning the plate with the cat's tail.

Luimneach a bhí,
  Baile Átha Cliath atá,
  Corcaigh a bheidh.

***

Spéir gan réiltín,
  Tinteán gan leanbh.

***

Bád gan stiúir nó cú gan eireaball.

***

Ansiúd a bádh a choileáin.

***

Is é an scéal é á insint don chapall is an capall ina
  chodladh.

***

Is leithide bualtrach satailt air.

***

## Cork

Limerick that was,
Dublin that is,
Cork that will be.

\*\*\*

A sky without a star,
A hearth without a child.

\*\*\*

Without a rudder a boat can't sail
And the hound can't run without its tail.

\*\*\*

'Twas there his pups drowned.[50]

\*\*\*

Telling a story
To a horse that's snoring.[51]

\*\*\*

Cowdung spreads when you walk on it.[52]

\*\*\*

---

[50] Said of someone in his habitual haunt, such as the local pub: the mother of pups frequently visits the spot where they were drowned. Liam O'Flaherty's story, *Bás na Bó*, is an eloquent testimony to maternal instincts in animals. The proverb suggests that paternal instincts also exist!

[51] Said of a disinterested listener.

[52] Some things are best left unsaid.

Mairg gur beag leis Dia mar lón.

***

Ní hí an bhreáthacht a chuireann an corcán ag fiuchadh.

***

Seachain is ná taobhaigh,
  Is ná tabhair an t-aitheantas ar aon rud.

***

Fearr seanfhiacha na seanfhala.

***

Conas a bheadh an t-ubhaillín
  Ach mar a bheadh an t-abhaillín?

***

Gach éan mar a oiltear
  Agus an naosc san abar.

***

Tart madra lá báistí.

***

An té nach bhfuil tobac aige cacadh sé ina phíp,
  Arsa an fear nach raibh aon easpa air féin.

***

Woe to him for whom God is little sustenance.

***

Beauty won't boil the pot.

***

Be on your guard and don't take sides
  And on your life never sacrifice friends.

***

Better old debts than old grudges.

***

Could the apple be
  But as the apple tree?[53]

***

Every bird as it is brought up
  And the snipe in the mud.

***

The dog's thirst on a rainy day.[54]

***

### Put that in your pipe!

He who has no tobacco may he shit in his pipe,
  Said the grouch with his pouch full.

---

[53] Well, in these days of genetic engineering – who knows?

[54] When someone asks for a drink and it's not the thirst that's killing him.

THE WASP IN THE MUG

Lá breá ag do chairde – dod adhlacan!

\*\*\*

Go ndeine an diabhal dréimire de chnámh do dhroma
   Ag piocadh úll i ngairdín Ifrinn.

\*\*\*

Nar gheala do chac ort!

\*\*\*

Nílim im scoláire is ní háil liom a bheith…

\*\*\*

Gach Ultach ar an ngunna
   Gach Connachtach ar an bpíce
   Gach Laighneach ar an gcapall
   – Is iad rogha na bhfear na Muimhnigh.

\*\*\*

Cad é an bac le mála na scadán
   Boladh na scadán a bheith air?

\*\*\*

May your friends have a fine day – at your burial!

\*\*\*

May the devil make a ladder of your backbone
And pluck apples in the garden of hell!

\*\*\*

May your shit never lighten![55]

\*\*\*

### Scholars beware!

I'm not a scholar and have no wish to be…[56]

\*\*\*

### Provincial profiles

Every Ulsterman to his gun
Every Connaughtman to his pike
Every Leinsterman to his horse
– It's the Munsterman I like.

\*\*\*

What's wrong with a bag full of herring
That smells of herring?

\*\*\*

---

[55] Black heavy faeces is a sign of ill-health.

[56] That's what the fox is supposed to have said to the donkey, admitting that he didn't know what was written on the horse's hoof. The donkey was sure that he could decipher it and asked the horse to show him the hoof. Well, he got the hoof all right – and that was the end of him.

Ariú nach é an fear é an bairneach – mar a dúirt an
  madarua.

*\*\*\**

Cuir an sagart i lár an pharóiste.

*\*\*\**

Gealt a chuir tús leis an rince.

*\*\*\**

Seacht scadán díol bradáin,
    Seacht mbradán díol róin,
    Seacht róin díol muice mara,
    Seacht muca mara díol míl mhóir,
    Seacht míol mhóra díol an cheannruáin chróin,
    Seacht gceannruáin chrón díol an domhain mhóir.

*\*\*\**

**Watch your tongue!**

Isn't the limpet some man, as the fox said.[57]

***

**The Priest**

Put the priest in the middle of the parish.[58]

***

A loon invented dancing.[59]

***

Seven herrings: A meal for a salmon,
  Seven salmon: A meal for a seal,
  Seven seals: A meal for a porpoise,
  Seven porpoises: A meal for a whale,
  Seven whales: A meal for a smooth blenny,
  Seven smooth blennies: A meal for the whole world.

***

---

[57] The limpet was on a rock, as is his wont, one sunny day. Along came the fox and thought he'd enjoy a little delicacy. He slipped his tongue under the half-open shell. The limpet closed tightly. The tide came in and drowned the fox.

[58] The 'priest' concerned here is a basket of boiled potatoes set in the middle of the floor for all to share. By the way, *sagairtín* can mean a little priest or an inedible periwinkle! Irish is notorious for the variety of applications of words which look and sound alike. Thus, *gealach* is the word for moon, or a thin slice of turnip. Dineen's Dictionary is a treasure-trove of such multiple meanings, layered upon one another. For instance *donn* is the colour brown, also the heart of a tree, also a prince, also 'the name of a fairy inhabiting sandbanks off the Clare coast'!

[59] *Rince* is from the English 'ring', as in ring-dances. Curiously, there was no native Irish word for dancing.

Scil Dhiarmada i gcac na ngabhar,
A d'ith iad in áit airní!

The skill of Diarmuid who, everybody knows,
Ate goat-droppings – thinking they were sloes![60]

---

[60] One could use this when your partner for dinner wonders what may be edible
or merely decorative.

Éisteacht na muice bradaí
  D'aireodh sí an féar ag fás.

***

Lia gach boicht bás.

***

Maireann croí éadrom i bhfad.

***

Is teoide don bhrat a dhúbladh.

***

Má thugann tú iasacht do chuid brístí
  Ná gearr na cnaipí díobh.

***

Is doiligh stocaí a bhaint d'fhear coslomnocht.

***

Is minic táilliúir agus drochthreabhsar air,
  Is minic gréasaí agus drochbhróga faoi.

***

Is mór orlach de shrón duine.

***

The thieving pig has ears on its ass
   And she can hear the growing grass.

\*\*\*

Death is every poor man's physician.

\*\*\*

The heart that's light lives long.

\*\*\*

The blanket's warmer when doubled.

\*\*\*

If you're going to lend your trousers
   Don't rip off the buttons.

\*\*\*

It's hard to take the stockings off a barefoot man.

\*\*\*

Many's the tailor with a bad pair of trousers,
   Many's the cobbler with a bad pair of shoes.

\*\*\*

An inch is a lot on a nose.[61]

\*\*\*

---

[61] Suitable as a motto on the wall in a plastic surgeon's waiting-room.

Rud ar bith leis an ocras a mhaolú, arsa an táilliúir agus
é ag ithe míoltóige.

\*\*\*

An rud nach leigheasann im nó uisce beatha, níl leigheas
air.

\*\*\*

Is measa scríob sa lorga ná buille den tua sa cheathrú.

\*\*\*

. Is garbh mí na gcuach.

\*\*\*

Chomh díomhaoin le ladhraicín píobaire.

\*\*\*

Níl insan saol seo ach tréimhse mí-ámharach
Agus níl fhios ag éinne ó inniu go dtí amárach.

\*\*\*

Anything to assuage the hunger, said the tailor
  swallowing a midge.[62]

***

## Cure

If whiskey or butter don't work the cure
  Then nothing at all will – and that's for sure.

***

A scratch to the shin is worse than an axe to the thigh.

***

A month of squalls
  When the cuckoo calls.

***

As idle as a piper's little finger.

***

This life is only a period of sorrow
  And nobody knows from today to tomorrow.

***

[62] The tailor is a very popular figure in Irish folklore, almost as popular as the legendary Gobán Saor, the Master Stone-Mason. In our own time the most famous tailor was from Gúgán Barra and is immortalised in *The Tailor and Ansty* (Mercier Press). Once an eminent Cork sculptor came to do the Tailor's head. A neighbour called and declared that it was most unnatural for any man to have two heads! [The Tailor was a fine speaker untainted by Victorian attitudes to bodily functions and his outpourings got him into trouble with the puritan clergy and the cleric-ridden state censorship of the time.]

Rud is mó 'thit amach ariamh
  Ní raibh ann ach scéal naoi lá,
  Mar do thiocfadh scéal eile ina dhiaidh
  Do bhainfeadh an mheabhair as.

***

An té a luíonn le gadharaibh éireoidh le dearnaitibh!

***

Is fearr banlámh den lá ná dhá bhanlámh den óiche.

***

An rud nach binn le duine ní chluineann sé é.

***

Níor bhlais an bia nach mblaisfidh an bás.

***

Cuir an breac san eangach sula gcuire tú sa phota é.

***

## Nine-day wonder

The greatest thing that ever occurred
  Was only a nine-day wonder,
  Then another story stirred
  And tore it all asunder!

\*\*\*

## Fleas

He who lies down with dogs at his ease
  At morning will jump up – hopping with fleas!

\*\*\*

A cubit of day is worth two cubits of night.[63]

\*\*\*

What's not sweet to the ear
  We simply don't hear.

\*\*\*

He who eats will be eaten![64]

\*\*\*

Net the fish
  Before you serve the dish.[65]

---

[63] A warning against working late at night. The *banlámh* was an old Irish cloth measurement of 21 inches – in West Kerry 24 inches!

[64] Death.

[65] Or, as good old Mrs Beeton used to say in relation to hare soup – first catch your hare.

Is minic a mhaolaigh béile maith brón.

***

Cia mholfadh an ghé bhréan
    Mura molfadh sí í féin?

***

Ní cluintear in Ifreann ach fead mná agus blao circe.

***

Go dtí Lá San Dic,
    An lá nach dtig.

***

Cé phósfas an t-airgead, pósfaidh sé óinseach,
    Imeoidh an t-airgead, fanfaidh an óinseach.

***

Spur ar an gcois agus gan an chos ann
    Is gan d'anam sa chorp ach ar nós cúr na habhann.

### Good meal

Sorrows are never as real
  After a good meal.

***

### Filthy goose

The goose that looks like she has waded in swill,
  If she won't praise herself – who else will?

***

### Hell

Nothing is heard in the depths of hell
  But a woman whistling and the cackle of a hen.

***

Until St Dick's day
Which won't come your way.

***

### Money and marriage

Marry the money, and marry the twit:
The money will go – but not the dim-wit.

***

### Sic transit ...

The spur on the heel – but the heel was a dream
  And the soul in your body is but foam on a stream.

Murach m'athair
  Dhéanfainn cathair.

***

Smachtódh gach éinne drochbhean, ach an té a mbeadh
  sí aige.

***

Ná díol caora dhubh
  Ná ceannaigh caora dhubh
  Ná bí gan caora dhubh.

***

Níl coill ar bith gan brosna a loiscithe.

***

Druid le fear na bruíne agus gheobhaidh tú síocháin.

***

Cuairt an lao ar an athbhuaile.

***

## Oedipus complex

Were it not for my father – more is the pity!
I'd be well on my way to building a city.

\*\*\*

An unruly woman is easy to control
Except when she happens to be your own.[66]

\*\*\*

## The black sheep

Don't sell a black sheep
Don't buy a black sheep
Don't be without a black sheep.

\*\*\*

Any forest can be fired by its own kindling.[67]

\*\*\*

Face up to the trouble-maker and he'll leave you alone.

\*\*\*

## The auld sod

The calf's visit to the disused milking-place.[68]

\*\*\*

---

[66] Had there been more women employed gathering lore for the Folklore Commission we might have a more balanced war between the sexes.

[67] Every Achilles has a heel.

[68] Nostalgic visit home.

Súil iolair i gceo,
   Súil con i ngleann,
   Súil mná óige ar aonach.

## Sharp!

The eagle's eye in the mist,
   The hound's eye in the glen,
   The eyes of a girl on young men.[69]

---

[69] The overwhelming popularity of the triad form in Irish proverbiology greatly facilitated my introduction of the *haiku* form to Irish prosody. The triad is one of the oldest forms of native oral literature and to this day you can still hear dozens of them from the older generation of native speakers.

# THE WASP IN THE MUG

An ní nach bhfeiceann súil ní bhrónann croí.

***

Ní dhéanfadh an saol capall rása d'asal.

***

Is minic a bhíos fréamh cham ag crann díreach.

***

Níl sprid ná púca ar bith
  Gan fios a chúise 'ge.

***

Ná tabhair dod dhailtín cóir nach cuibhe dhó,
  Ná comhluadar le huaislibh tíre;
  Mura gcoinnír smachtaithe é is é 'choimeád foríseal
  Is measa le cothú é ná coileán mac tíre.

***

# THE WASP IN THE MUG

The heart does not grieve what the eye cannot perceive.

*\*\*\**

### Thoroughbred

Whatever else might come to pass
  You won't make a racehorse of an ass.

*\*\*\**

Many is the upright tree
  With a branch as crooked as can be.

*\*\*\**

### Why are we here?

There's not a spirit or a pooka in the air
  That doesn't know why he is there.

*\*\*\**

### Child-rearing

Keep him away from the company of gentry,
  Give him only what befits a child,
  If you don't keep him strict within the bounds of
    decency
  He'll be harder to rear than the wolves of the wild.

*\*\*\**

Bhéarfadh súgán cátha chun dlí thú
Is ní thabharfadh slabhra iarainn thar n-ais thú!

\*\*\*

Slaghdán Dhónaill
Slaghdán i gcónaí.

\*\*\*

Ba chuma Donncha um Nollaig nó thall faoi Cháisc
Mar bhí Nollaig ag Donncha oíche is lá.

\*\*\*

Níor chodail an dris chosáin riamh.

\*\*\*

Ochón ó! An t-éan a bhí ar an gcrann,
Nuair a d'imigh sé ní raibh sé ann.

\*\*\*

Ceann dubh ar gach maidin earraigh
Agus eireaball seannaigh as san siar.

\*\*\*

Ní thig meirg ar an eochair a mbaintear leas aisti.

\*\*\*

# THE WASP IN THE MUG

## Litigious

For a wisp of a straw
  To the court of law
  And an iron chain
  Couldn't drag you back again!

\*\*\*

Donald has a cold –
  He has that of old.

\*\*\*

Dennis at Christmas or Dennis at Easter
  One and the same – Dennis always a-feasting.

\*\*\*

All day, all night until dawn peeps,
  The wayside bramble never sleeps.[70]

\*\*\*

The bird on the tree, alas and alack!
  Once he flew off he never came back!

\*\*\*

Spring morning: head all black,
  Tail of a fox after that.

\*\*\*

The key that's used does not rust.

---

[70] Sources of annoyance on your path.

Seachain fearg ó fhear na foidhne.

***

Gach re mbliain 'bhíonn an fia fireann.

***

Fiach dubh fómhair nó fionnóg earraigh,
  Droch-chomhartha iad do bheith ag screadaigh.

***

Fuath dem fhuathaibh is cóir sin:
  Ridire gan scian aige ar cóisir,
  Fear liath d'iarraidh mná óige,
  Buachailleacht cois luaithe an tráthnóna.

***

Is minic a bhí droch-chrú faoi chapall gabhann.

***

Is minic a chealg briathra míne cailín críonna.

***

Ceann cíortha a dhíolas na cosa.

***

Beware the anger of the patient man.

\*\*\*

Every second year the deer is a male.[71]

\*\*\*

### Misfortune bodes

Autumn cormorant, scald-crow in spring
   For them to be screeching – an unlucky thing.

\*\*\*

All the hates that are easiest to understand:
   A knight without a knife at feasting time,
   A grey-haired man seeking a young girl's hand,
   At watch over ashes at evening time.

\*\*\*

Many is the blacksmith's horse badly shod.

\*\*\*

### Honeyed words

Many a girl lost what can't be bought with money –
   And all because of words, sprinkled with honey.

\*\*\*

Comb your hair and you're half-way there.[72]

---

[71] Offspring.

[72] Good grooming compensates for many defects.

# THE WASP IN THE MUG

Is fuar an rud clú gan chara.

***

An té a chailleas a chlú cailleann a náire.

***

Is minic a bhí cú mall sona.

***

Moill ar tí an deabhaidh.

***

Is mairg a mbeadh doicheall roimh dheacair aige.

***

Ding de féin a scoilteas an leamhán.

***

Ná déan acht agus ná bris acht.

***

Fame and glory – how terribly cold
  If there's no hand to hold.

\*\*\*

Lose your good name and you'll lose all shame.

\*\*\*

### Better late than never

Many a lagging dog came home – to find a bone.

\*\*\*

As fast as you can go
  It will only make you slow.[73]

\*\*\*

If with difficulties he should meet –
  Woe to him who sounds the retreat.

\*\*\*

A wedge of its own timber splits the elm.[74]

\*\*\*

Don't make a decree, don't break a decree.[75]

\*\*\*

---

[73] Festina lente.

[74] Diamond cut diamond.

[75] Follow traditional ways.

An té a mbíonn an t-ádh ar maidin air bíonn sé air
maidin agus tráthnóna.

\*\*\*

Ná baintear an t-ainm den bhlonag.

\*\*\*

Is maith an t-anlann an t-ocras.

\*\*\*

Is fearr bail ná iomad.

\*\*\*

Níor tháinig riamh an mheidhir mhór nach dtiocfadh
ina diaidh an dobrón.

\*\*\*

Is díon an crann fad is díon dó féin é.

\*\*\*

Briseann an dúchas trí chrúba an chait.

\*\*\*

If you're in luck at the break of day
All day long your luck will stay.[76]

\*\*\*

## Call a spade a spade

If it's fat – call it that!

\*\*\*

If it's hunger you feel –
That's sauce on your meal.

\*\*\*

Enough is better than too much.

\*\*\*

There never was pure joy without alloy.

\*\*\*

A tree will give you shelter as long as it shelters itself.[77]

\*\*\*

Nature, following its own laws,
Breaking out in the cat's paws.

\*\*\*

---

[76] Begin well – end well.

[77] Until it becomes saturated.

# THE WASP IN THE MUG

Ag cuimilt saille de thóin na muice méithe.

Rubbing fat on the fleshy pig's arse.[78]

<hr>

[78] Superfluous additions! The pig is an important character in oral and written literature. It occurs plentifully in place-names, such as Ros Muc, the peninsula of pigs. The Irish are inordinately fond of bacon. The sacred druidic tree of pre-Christian times was the oak. Pigs ate of the fruit of the oak, acorns and, by symbiosis, were themselves sacred.

Folaíonn grá gráin.

\*\*\*

Is geal leis an bhfiach dubh a ghearrcach féin.

\*\*\*

Is fearr bothán lán ná caisleán mór folamh.

\*\*\*

Is leor don dreoilín a nead.

\*\*\*

Buíochas do Dhia is do Mhuire,
  Ach mura bhfuair mé go leor
  Fuair mé oiread is duine eile.

\*\*\*

Más crúsca thú seachain an corcán.

\*\*\*

Ná bíodh aon chat ach cat a mharós luch.

\*\*\*

Ag cur claí timpeall goirt leis an gcuach a choinneáil
  istigh.

Love veils the unlovely.

***

The raven thinks its nestling
  Is a bright thing!

***

Better the hovel of plenty
  Than the castle that's empty.

***

The nest of the wren is as much as it needs.

***

**Thank God!**

Thanks be to God and His holy mother,
  If I didn't get a lot, I got as much as the other!

***

A jug should not consort with a pot.

***

Let's have no cat in the house
That will not catch a mouse.

***

Fencing the field to keep in the cuckoo.

Is maol gualainn gan bhráthair.

\*\*\*

Ní heolas go haontíos, ní haontíos go pluid, ní pluid go
bliain.

\*\*\*

Is uaigneach an níochán nach mbíonn léine ann!

\*\*\*

Is fearr rith maith ná drochsheasamh.

\*\*\*

Tabhair an mhóin abhaile agus cuirfidh mé tine mhór
síos.

\*\*\*

Dhá ní gan náire, tart is grá, ach thug an tochas an barr
leis.

\*\*\*

Ní bheathaíonn na briathra na bráithre.

\*\*\*

Grá don chomhluadar a thugas na gadhair chuig an
Aifreann.

A shoulder is bare
  Without a brother's hand to care.

***

To know me? Live with me my dear
  And share my blanket, at least for a year.

***

That laundry is sad – not a shirt to be had!

***

Better to run while you can
  Than stand like a man.

***

You fetch the turf and I'll light the fire.

***

### Scratching

No shame being thirsty, or making love –
  But scratching? Heavens above!

***

Fables won't fatten the friars.

***

With an hour or two to pass
  The dogs come to Mass.

Is é an madarua is túisce a fhaigheann boladh a bhroma féin.

## Fart

The fox is the first to smell his own fart.

An coileach ag déanamh cothrom na Féinne i measc na
gcearc.

\*\*\*

Níl tuile dá mhéad nach dtránn.

\*\*\*

An t-aonú aithne dhéag – tabhair aire duit féin.

\*\*\*

Síoda buí ar Shiobhán agus gioblachaí ar a hathair.

\*\*\*

Is éasca dhá shimléar a dhéanamh ná tine a choinneáil i
gceann acu.

\*\*\*

Trí rud nach raibh riamh ann:
  Nead ag luich i gcluais cait
  Giorria i seid con
  Gé ar gor i bpluais madarua.

\*\*\*

Trí shaghas inchinne:
  Inchinn reatha
  Inchinn chloiche
  Inchinn chéarach.

The cockerel cherishing his hens equally.

***

No matter how great
  The flood will abate.

***

The eleventh commandment – look after yourself.

***

There's Siobhán in her silks of gold
  And there is her father, raggedy and cold.

***

Easier to build two chimneys than keep a fire going in
  one of them.

***

Three things that never have been:
  A mouse's nest in a cat's ear
  A hare in the hound's kennel
  A hatching goose in a fox's den.

***

### Brains!

Three types of mind:
  The volatile mind
  The mind of stone
  The mind of wax.[79]

---

[79] Wax here denotes 'retentive'.

Trí trioblóidí mhná na Rinne:
    Páistí
    Prátaí
    Is truscar!

***

Trí nithe chuaigh de Harry Stottle a thuiscint:
    Intinn na mban
    Obair na mbeach
    Agus teacht is imeacht na taoide.

***

Súil, glúin, uille – na trí rud is leochailí.

***

Dá mba ór an duille donn thíolacfadh Fionn é.

***

Doras feasa fiafraí.

***

The women of Ring are troubled indeed:
  Children
  Potatoes
  Cast-up sea-weed![80]

\*\*\*

### It's that man Harry Stottle again!

Aristotle was stumped by these:
  The mind of a woman
  The ebb and flow of the tide
  The work of the bees.

\*\*\*

The easiest to hurt are these three:
  The eye
  The elbow
  And the knee.

\*\*\*

### Gold

If the autumn leaves were gold, Fionn would give it
  away.[81]

\*\*\*

Questioning is the door to knowledge.

---

[80] Ring is a beautiful sea-side area in Co. Waterford where some Irish is still spoken, in a very distinctive dialect. It produced such luminaries as poet Áine Ní Fhoghlú, singer Nioclás Tóibín and Seán Ó Cuirrín who translated *Dracula* into mellifluous Irish.

[81] Fionn MacCumhaill, the mythical Celtic figure who gave his name to Wien/Vienna.

Ní ghabhann dorn dúnta seabhac.

\*\*\*

Turas na gcearc go Críoch Lochlann.

\*\*\*

Ní i gcónaí a mharaíonn daidín fia.

\*\*\*

An luibh ná fachtar a fhóineann.

\*\*\*

Ní dhíolann dearmad fiacha.

\*\*\*

Uaisle éisteas le healaín.

\*\*\*

Trí nithe is sia ina bhfanann a rian:
    Rian guail i gcoill
    Rian siséil i líg
    Agus rian soic i gcrích.

\*\*\*

A closed hand doesn't catch a hawk.

***

It's the hens' journey to Scandinavia.[82]

***

Daddy doesn't always kill a deer.[83]

***

The herb that cures is the one that can't be found.

***

Forgetting does not repay a debt.

***

It's a sign of nobility to patronise the arts.[84]

***

Three things which leave the longest-lasting traces:
    Trace of charcoal on wood
    Trace of chisel on stone
    Trace of ploughshare on furrow.

***

---

[82] No chance of going back again. It was believed that the Vikings brought hens to Ireland.

[83] Cause for a minor celebration.

[84] Said by some poor poet or other ... well, he would, wouldn't he!

Ní fios cé is túisce craiceann na seanchaorach nó na caorach óige ar an bhfraith.

***

Ná gearradh do theanga do scornach.

***

Beirbh birín dom is beireod birín duit.

***

Ní cuimhnítear ar an arán a itear.

***

Deacair giorria a chur as tor nach mbeidh sé.

***

Ní baintear fuil as tornapa.

***

Fearr le himirt féin ná mac le hól.

***

Súil le cúiteamh a lomann an cearrbhach.

***

One can't say whether the skin of the old sheep or that of the young sheep will be the first to hang from the rafter.

\*\*\*

Let your tongue not cut your throat.

\*\*\*

Cook a *birín* for me and I'll cook one for you.[85]

\*\*\*

Eaten bread is not remembered.

\*\*\*

### The hare that wasn't there!

Difficult to drive a hare out of a bush if he's not in it.

\*\*\*

Blood is not drawn from a turnip.

\*\*\*

Better a son given to gambling than to drink.

\*\*\*

The next 'good thing' ruins the gambler.

\*\*\*

---

[85] Birín is a diminutive of bior rósta, a roasting spit.

Is fearr an t-imreas ná an t-uaigneas.

Rather strife
  Than a lonely life.

Beag sochar na síormheisce.

***

Bean ar meisce, pis in aisce.

***

Maith an mustard an sliabh.

***

Is luachmhar an t-anam, mar a dúirt an táilliúir agus é
ag rith ón ngandal.

***

Muca ciúine a itheann triosc.

***

Sroichfidh each mall muilleann.

***

Cad a dhéanfadh mac an chait ach luch a mharú.

***

Déanann codladh fada tóin leis an duine.

***

Little profit in being constantly pissed!

\*\*\*

Drunken woman, free ride.[86]

\*\*\*

The mountain is a good mustard.[87]

\*\*\*

Life is precious, as the tailor said fleeing from the gander.

\*\*\*

## Hogwash!

Still swine guzzle hogwash.

\*\*\*

A slow horse will reach the mill.

\*\*\*

What would the cat's son do but kill a mouse.

\*\*\*

Sleep long and you'll have no arse to your trousers.[88]

---

[86] *Pis* is the Irish for vagina and also, because of a resemblance, a pea-pod.

[87] Appetiser.

[88] *Leis,* in Irish, can mean: 'also', 'a thigh', 'of his' and 'naked' so that *'bhí leis leis leis leis'* translates as 'a thigh of his was also bare'.

Bíonn cosa crua ar chapall iasachta.

\*\*\*

Is beag an dealg a dhéanfadh braon.

\*\*\*

Níor dhún Dia doras riamh nár oscail sé ceann eile.

\*\*\*

An bhean atá dóighiúil is furasta a cóiriú.

\*\*\*

Éist mórán agus can beagán.

\*\*\*

Is taibhseach iad adharca na mbó thar lear.

\*\*\*

Meileann muilte Dé go mall.

\*\*\*

Is olc an t-éan a shalaíonn a nead féin.

\*\*\*

A borrowed horse is hard of foot.[89]

\*\*\*

The tiniest thorn can suppurate.

\*\*\*

God never closes one door without opening another.

\*\*\*

A handsome woman is easily dressed.

\*\*\*

Hear much, say little.

\*\*\*

Foreign cows have long horns.[90]

\*\*\*

God's mill grinds slow.

\*\*\*

It's a bad bird that fouls its own nest.

\*\*\*

---

[89] Borrowing can lead to abuse.

[90] Distance lends enchantment to a view.

Ní hé lá na gaoithe lá na scolb.

\*\*\*

Is olc an chearc nach scríobann di féin.

\*\*\*

Tosach sláinte codladh.

\*\*\*

Tuar an t-ádh agus tiocfaidh sé!

\*\*\*

Ag caitheamh an tsaoil is an saol ár gcaitheamh.

\*\*\*

Paidir chapaill.

\*\*\*


Is mairg a d'imreadh a mháthair orthu.

\*\*\*

Is fuirist gabháil thar dhoras duine mhairbh
Nuair ná bionn sé féin ná a mhadra istigh.

\*\*\*

## Scollops!

The windy day is no day for scollops.[91]

\*\*\*

It's a poor hen that won't scratch for herself.

\*\*\*

Sleep is the first sign of recovery.

\*\*\*

Predict good fortune and it will come!

\*\*\*

We consume time while she consumes us.

\*\*\*

A horse's prayer.[92]

\*\*\*

## Bad hand at cards

Woe to him who'd bet his mother on them!

\*\*\*

It is easy to pass the dead man's door
When himself and his dog aren't there anymore.

---

[91] The scollop is a looped stick for securing thatch on a roof.

[92] Endless rigmarole. The ploughing horse that stumbled on his knees spent a long time thus – as if in prayer.

Na trí ní is mó giodam:
  Piscín cait
  Meannán gabhair
  Nó baintreach óg mhná.

*\*\**

Bainne as diaidh feola agus uisce as diaidh éisc.

*\*\**

D'íosfadh sé an gharbhach.

*\*\**

Is trom an t-ualach putóga folmha.

*\*\**

Bia rí ruacain
  Bia buachalla bairnigh
  Bia caillí miongáin
  Is í á bpiocadh le snáthaid.

*\*\**

## THE WASP IN THE MUG

### Frisky!

The three friskiest things:
  The kitten
  The kid goat
  The young widow.

***

Milk after meat and water after fish.[93]

***

He'd eat the robin-run-the-hedge.[94]

***

Empty intestines are a heavy load.

***

### Alive alive-o!

Cockles food for a king
  Limpets food for a youth
  Food for old hags periwinkles
  And they picking them with a pin.

---

[93] The traditionally preferred drink with meat and fish respectively. When the potato took over in pre-famine Ireland much lore about food and hundreds of recipes were lost to later generations. Does anybody know today how the vegetable dish, *sancam soncam,* was prepared? Has anybody today tasted bread made from acorn flour? Were shamrocks used as a salad ingredient? Why did well-known lunatics, such as Suibhne Geilt (Mad Sweeney), have a preference for watercress? Those early Gaelic Leaguers who hoped for a revival of the ancestral language, traditional music, dress and so on, seem to have overlooked food!

[94] He'd eat anything at all. Robin-run-the-hedge is also known as cleavers or clivers, or goose-grass. Very prickly.

A bhuachaill, beir buartha go bpósfair
  Is an uair sin beir buartha do dhóthain!

*****

Cion gan fhios do mhnaoi nó leanbh.

*****

An chéad ghrá mná agus an dara grá fir.

*****

Bod seanduine nó cíoch seanmhná.

*****

Is minic a bheir dall ar ghiorria.

*****

Ná feic a bhfeicir
  Is ná clois a gcloisir
  Is má fiafraítear díot
  Abair ná feadrais.

*****

Boy, you'll be troubled till you're married –
And then you'll be properly harried![95]

***

Love unbeknown to woman or child.[96]

***

A woman's first love, a man's second love.[97]

***

An old man's penis, an old woman's breast.[98]

***

Many's the blind man caught a hare.[99]

***

Hear not what you hear
See not what you see
And if you're asked
Say 'Don't ask me!'

***

---

[95] At least the Brehon Laws allowed for divorce and listed among unnatural cruelties – giving grounds for divorce – excessive wind in one's partner's intestines.

[96] If women or children know that they are loved they will take advantage of it.

[97] These are the most enduring.

[98] Drooping – God save the mark! Given the natural curiosity that children have about sex it's amazing how few children know the Irish for 'penis' – a reflection on the unnatural sterilised manner in which the language has been taught in schools. Words for 'penis' include: *toilfhéith, slat, bod, crann, pilbín, an fear bán, an ball fearga* and a boy's penis is *sceidín*!

[99] A sarcastic proverb when you don't believe a word of someone's boasting.

Níor loisc seanchat é féin riamh.

An old cat never scorched himself.

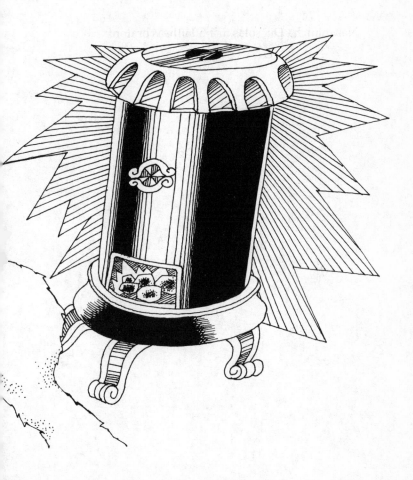

Cosa gloine fúibh is go mbrise siad!

\*\*\*

Dioc ort!

\*\*\*

Nár mhúcha Dia solas na bhflaitheas orainn!

\*\*\*

Glass legs under you – and may they break![100]

\*\*\*

Pip on you![101]

\*\*\*

May God not quench the light of heaven on us![102]

\*\*\*

---

[100] Said to hens!

[101] Pip is a disease in poultry, hawks etc. Thus the expression 'he gives me the pip!'

[102] Said on putting out the light.

## ANOTHER INTERESTING TITLE
## FROM MERCIER PRESS

# '... *Before the Devil Knows You're Dead*'
### *Irish Blessings, Toasts and Curses*

## Padraic O'Farrell

Hearing news of a death or marriage, consoling neighbours in sorrow or sharing their joy, looking for a husband or wife, saving turf or going fishing – Irish people had blessings and curses for every occasion.

> \* *'May you be in heaven an hour before the devil knows you're dead'*

> \* *'May God give you luck and put a good man in your way, and if he is not good, may the wedding whiskey be drunk at his wake.'*

> \* *'May today be the first day of the best years of your life.'*

> \* *'When the road rises to meet you may it slap you in the face.'*

> \* *'May you be plagued with an itch and no nails to scratch.'*

> \* *'May the wind always be at your back.'*

The above is just a sample from the blessings and curses collected by Padraic O'Farrell in this book. Luckily many of the old sayings have survived. A few startling new ones have been added too!